Weston-super-Mare
The Sands of Time

Acknowledgments and special thanks to:

My parents, Bob and Carmel Keyes

Graham and Elizabeth Davis

Robert and Elizabeth Keyes

Patrick and Nora O'Connell

Jeffrey Archer

Brian Heath

Martin Taylor

Bob Acland

Dennis Jones

Brian Austin

. . . and all others who have helped with this book

Weston-super-Mare
The Sands of Time

Anthony Keyes

Published by Sigma Leisure - an imprint of
Sigma Press, 1 South Oak Lane, Wilmslow, Cheshire SK9 6AR, England.

British Library Cataloguing in Publication Data: A CIP record for this book is available from the British Library.

ISBN: 1-85058-470-2

Typesetting and Design by: Sigma Press, Wilmslow, Cheshire.

Edited by: Graham Beech

Printed by: Manchester Free Press

Cover design: Manchester Free Press

Cover photograph: Weston-super Mare's Grand Pier. Paddling children feature on this original and rare colour postcard sent from Weston to Thornbury, Bristol, at 10.30am on 13th July, 1905.

Foreword

This book is a treasure trove of memories. Its original postcards and photographs reveal nearly a hundred years of Weston-super-Mare's history. From the pomp and grandeur of the Victorian and Edwardian age through to the present day, the fine photographs and text draw one back into rich remembrances, happy times and sudden drama.

Weston-super-Mare, one of the most famous seaside resorts in the country, and certainly to my mind, by far the best, is remembered by millions. Who can look through this book without feeling a sudden excitement when catching sight of some mistily remembered detail, face or view?

Weston is surely the jewel in Somerset's crown, and the chance to look at the town of my childhood, its grand buildings, fine people and superb scenery has been enormously fascinating and pleasurable for me. There is one thing of which we can be certain: Weston may have changed, but our strong and enduring memories can't be taken away. In another hundred years nostalgia will still be in fashion and Weston-super-Mare will still be providing millions of people with real pleasure and the sense of a life well lived.

In the future, Weston-super-Mare, through the efforts and care of its businesses, people and leaders, can be sure to flourish and prosper. It is a town that I, along with countless others, hold in deep affection and it is that shared love, above all else, that guarantees its future.

I spent the first eighteen years of my life in Weston-super-Mare and I am left with many happy memories. I began my education at Christchurch Primary School where I ended up as Milk Monitor and Bell Ringer. The Headmaster was Mr Holcombe who as Mayor of the town gave me my first interest in local politics. Although I went away to Wellington to continue my schooling I still have vivid memories of my holidays in Weston when I lived with my mother and father in a small flat in South Road.

My lasting recollections are of the Somerset Cricket Festival, even though during that period of my life it was rare, almost memorable, for Somerset to win a County match. I recall fish and chips purchased from Coffins and Walls Ice Cream ("more than a treat – a food"), which I sold on the Weston sands as a holiday job. Then there was Baker's Coaches taking you to exciting places like Burnham, Bridgwater and Bristol and not to mention the Grand Pier where one old penny could keep you occupied on a slot machine for a whole hour. Do you remember the farthing?

I return regularly to the town to see my mother, who still lives in Uphill and I always come back to London thinking how lucky I was to be brought up in the West Country. I hope all of you who read this book will gain an insight and understanding as to why we Westonians feel we began our life somewhere special.

Jeffrey Archer

The Lord Archer of Weston-super-Mare

" . . . the Grand Pier where one old penny could keep you occupied on a slot machine for a whole hour"

A Mayoral Message . . .

It gives me great pleasure as Town Mayor of Weston-super-Mare to write a short introduction to "Weston-super-Mare – The Sands of Time".

Weston-super-Mare developed as a Victorian seaside resort, although a village had existed here since mediaeval times and the Manor of Weston-super-Mare was created in 1216. The village nestled under the brow of Worlebury Hill, itself the site of an immense Iron Age encampment. There were three important buildings above the flood level – the Church, the Rectory and the Manor House – with the remainder of the village straddling from West Street, along High Street as far as Regent Street. The villagers were mainly engaged in farming and fishing.

Following the opening of the Royal Hotel in 1810 and the commencement of a coach service, people began to visit Weston-super-Mare, thus establishing the town as a seaside resort, and the population (which had remained around 100 for centuries) began to increase. By the year 1820 Weston-super-Mare had become a fashionable resort and the increase in visitors assisted the development of facilities in the town.

The nineteenth Century brought with it tremendous change, particularly with the advent of mass transport. Isambard Kingdom Brunel built his railway to Weston-super-Mare in 1841 and the town "took off", firstly as a health resort, with the development of medicinal baths on Knightstone Island, but, more importantly, as a tourist centre.

Between the years 1840 – 1870 there was a rapid growth in the population with the development of the railway being an important factor as Weston-super-Mare was one of the first resorts to have a railway link. The building work escalated and the development of the town increased rapidly from 1841 onwards.

By 1937 Weston-super-Mare had grown tremendously and King George VI granted a Charter of Incorporation creating the Borough of Weston-super-Mare with the inauguration of the First Charter Mayor, Henry Butt, and the Weston-super-Mare Borough Council.

1974 saw Local Government reorganisation, as a result of which Weston-super-Mare (with a population of some 50,000) lost Borough status and became the "Town of Weston-super-Mare within the District of Woodspring in the newly formed County of Avon".

Weston-super-Mare now has a population approaching 70,000 and, in 1992, a further review of local government commenced. Under this review it was anticipated that the County of Avon and the District of Woodspring will be abolished. If the Local Government Commission's present recommendations are supported by the local populace and accepted by the Secretary of State, out of the ashes will rise a new unitary authority "North West Somerset" within the historic County of Somerset.

Brian Heath

Councillor Brian Heath. Inaugurated as Town Mayor of Weston-super-Mare on 19th May 1994.

"... people began to visit Weston-super-Mare, thus establishing the town as a seaside resort"
— an early view of The Sands

Contents

The Time... The Place...

The 150th Anniversary of Weston-super-Mare becoming a town was celebrated in 1992. Weston is in historic Somerset, only 20 miles from Bristol with good road access via the M5 motorway. It has three railway stations: the main one is in the heart of the town and, leaving in the direction of Bristol, there is Weston Milton station and Worle Parkway, which opened on 24th September 1990.

Weston Bay, with its long sweep of flat sandy beach, is situated on the south side of the Bristol Channel immediately opposite Cardiff on the Welsh coast. *The Westonian* guide published in 1829 describes the beach as follows: "The shore is so nearly level, that at ebb tide, a stranger would suppose that the sea had abandoned the place; but at full tide, the effect is fine". During the summer months, the beach comes into its own when the tide recedes.

At the height of summer, Weston, with its glorious sunsets, sea breezes and golden sands can seem like paradise. Westonians and holiday-makers can be seen walking along the promenade taking in the ozone from the fresh air which blows direct from the Atlantic Ocean. The power of the sea is, however, never to be underestimated. Changing climatic conditions of Weston's past history have seen storms rage against the shore with tremendous violence. A sea wall spanning the length of the sea front protects the town.

Weston-super-Mare — The Birth of the Town

The Weston Improvement and Market Act was passed in Parliament on 13 May 1842 and, as a result of this Act, Weston became a town. The Act provided for "paving, lighting, watching, cleansing and otherwise improving the town ... and for establishing a market" and, in order to pay for these services, Weston's first town commissioners had the power to levy rates.

A few years earlier, the Parliamentary Act of 1838 gave Weston a branch railway line and station and the first service began on 14 June 1841. Weston is on a branch line from the main Bristol to Exeter route and the first carriages to pull into Weston station were horse-drawn, but these were often so slow — especially with a head wind — that many visitors preferred to walk!

It was not until 1850 that a steam train was used. Weston became one of the first seaside resorts in the world to have a rail link. A separate goods station was built in the 1860s and in 1866 a larger passenger terminal opened with an excursion platform for day-trippers. The present station was built in 1884.

The first few pages of this book illustrate Weston's early days, starting with its West Country origins and through its early days as a seaside resort.

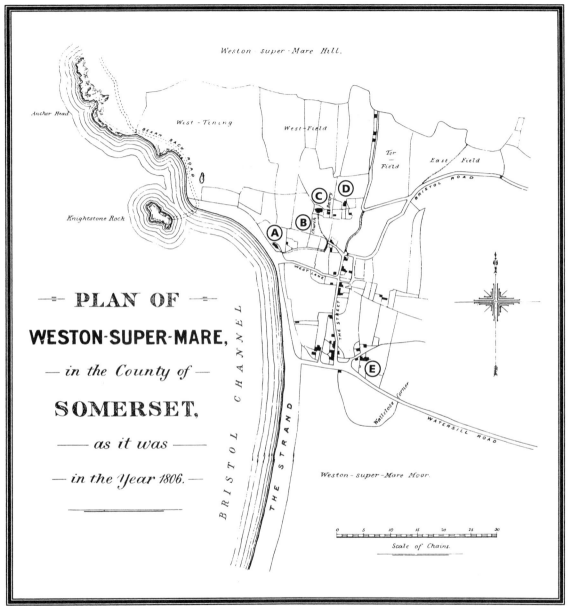

Weston as it was

An 1806 plan of Weston. The 1801 Census recorded just '105 souls'. Marked on the map are:

[A] Leeves Cottage

[B] The Parish Church

[C] The Rectory

[D] The Manor House, also known as Grove House, home of Rev Wadham Pigott.

[E] Farmer King's old farmhouse

These are referred to in the text of this book.

Old Weston and 'Zumerzet' Dialect

In 1826, a visitor from London came to Weston, staying at the Old Farm House which stood on today's Alexandra Parade corner of Orchard Place. The farmer was a widower with two children, Matthew and Hannah. He remarried a widow named Hurst, who had four children of her own, John, George, Sarah and Elizabeth. They later had three more children: George, Silvester and Joseph – making nine in all! An account of the visit was described in 'The Old Farm House' by Charlotte Eleanor Wilson, published in 1882.

This is how Charlotte Wilson described her accommodation requirements as the London visitor: "Come all the way from Lunnun to Bath, and from Bath to Wesson! What wull 'em do? 'Here you, Zue," said the Dame, "go wi' 'em to Varmer King's and ax him if he'd like to have 'em. Tell him they be people from Lunnun, and nobody'll have 'em."

Interestingly, Farmer King's property became the site of the first offices of 'The Westonian' – now the Weston and Somerset Mercury – which was first published on 1st April 1843.

The Old Farm House. The land included Meadow Lane (now Meadow Street).

The Somerset dialect spoken to the 'Lunnun' visitor has changed over the years. On the next page, there is a sample conversation between the the farmer's wife and Hannah – see what you make of it:

The London Visitor

13

SOMERSETSHIRE DIALOGUES.

—➤➤➤❮❮❮—

Dialogue the First.

FARMER'S WIFE.—Come, zit down by the vire, and have a cup of tea wi' I. I wull stir him up a bit: (seeing the poker in the fire) thic poker wull be burnt to deeth. They wull always leave he sticking in the vire, zay what you wull. Have zome toasted cheeze; doant zay noa. Hannah, wull ye have a cup of tea?

HANNAH. Noa, A'nt; I likes bacon and taters best.

WIFE. Zo does my old man; he ha'e had bacon, taters, and zider for his breakvast, vor these vive-and-twenty years; but I likes a cup o' tea bezide.

HANNAH. Doant you, Miss, ha'e bacon and taters vor breakvast in Lunnun?

VISITOR. No, Hannah.

HANNAH. Nor toasted cheeze?

VISITOR. Never. I even dislike the smell of cheese in the morning.

HANNAH. Moi heart!—and I do think it zsmells zo nice!

FARMER *without, driving the ducks from the garden.*

FARMER. Shew!—shew!—geet out!—geet out! I wish zomebody would zsteal thic old woman's dookes!

Old Varmer King . . .

. . . and Hannah, the Varmer's Niece

Zum more to zay . . .

Everyday items in the farmhouse were talked about in the old dialect. The glossary provided by Charlotte Wilson is invaluable!

Thic Table wants only zom. Wood or Zstones put under the Legs, and then he wull zstand zstraight.

The Worms ha'e yeaten the Voot off he.

The Legs o' thic Chair ha'e been zo vor years. Doan't lean back in he, or you'll vall.

CANDLE 16 TO THE POUND

Did ye never zee zuch zmall Candles bevore? I call him a big one. What we burn are vour -and-twenty to the Pound.

I uze he vor a Roling Pin when I make a Pie.

Thic Crime Jug has lost the Handle, zo has the Coffee Pot.—Ye must lay hold of he at the top wi' a great lump of Rag when ye pours the Coffee out.

GLOSSARY.

Thic,—used for this, that, those, and these.
Z for S,—as zun for sun ; Zarah for Sarah.
V for F,—as, vall down for fall down ; vive for five.
He for every article of furniture.
Draaing off for drawing off.
Multiplying Glass for magnifying glass.

Only zee how they've took the Edges off the Knives wi' cutting Wood wi'em.

Thic Knife won't stop in the Handle.

Thic Vork turns round in his.

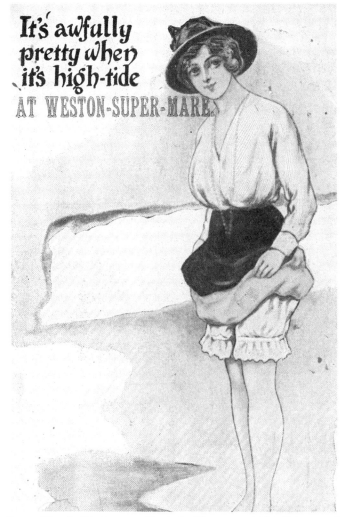

Ozone Friendly: Weston-super-Mare's front line was, and still is, its long sandy flat beach. This card was written on a Saturday at 4.15 pm and posted at 6.15 pm 26 July 1919 to Redcliffe, Bristol. Twenty years earlier, Bathing Machines existed in Weston until the early 1900s. Ladies' machines were in Glentworth Bay and the men's in front of the Grand Atlantic on the beach. Many were destroyed after the storm in September 1903 and never replaced.

A 1908 view of the church of St Nicholas at Uphill, described in 1826 as a well-known landmark for sailors, being frequently white-washed and making it conspicuous for many miles around. It was built on a bleak and exposed hilltop, rather than the valley below, where the building was said to have started. Seemingly, each day's work on the new church in the valley was mysteriously undone during the night. The building materials found themselves carried to the summit of the hill, which led the locals to believe that St Nicholas, the patron saint of sailors, preferred a hill-top site as a better landmark for mariners.

The Promenade, Weston-super-Mare. A postcard that was sent at 7.30 pm on 22 March 1907 from Weston to Bath. Note the use of the sunshades and hats, even by children.

Entrance to Woods, Weston-super-Mare. The entrance to the woods in this early view is via the sea front, by Birnbeck Pier. The woods were originally the property of the Smyth-Pigott family who gave free access to the area; later, the land passed to the Borough Council who preserved it for future generations. The track entrance on this postcard is above the rocky foreshore.

Weston's only Toll Road, at Kewstoke. The road runs between Weston and Kewstoke. Pictured in 1993, the daily return charge was 45p for cars and vans. Season tickets for Kewstoke residents were £3.50 per annum but for Woodspring residents the charge was £4.50 per annum.

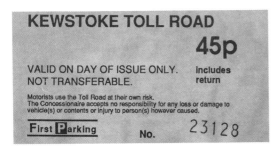

Ticket for the Kewstoke Toll Road

The Victorian Royal Mail wall post box on Arundell Road, Weston-super-Mare.

Weston's original pre-Victorian heritage can be found in various parts of the town, as shown in this picture of The Thatched Cottage Restaurant. This stands on Weston-super-Mare's sea front and it dates from Weston's original antiquity, unlike the nearby shadow of the 1970 multi-storey Weston College building. Pictured here on 13 February 1993, this same building is still known as Leeves Cottage to this day, though it is currently a restaurant. It is unusual to see a thatched roof on Weston sea front and this is above the oldest part of the building, now the grill room of the restaurant. Visitors take advantage of the improved patio area, while enjoying the summer sunshine. In 1791, Reverend William Leeves built the original residence for himself, as a summer cottage on the sand dunes! He was the Vicar of Wrington for 40 years. In 1854, the buildings caught fire and were badly damaged.

Piers and Shipping

Birnbeck Pier was constructed in 1867. The sea and storms have taken their toll on the structure. Cecil Smyth-Pigott laid the foundation stone in 1864 and the pier was opened on 5th June 1867. The "Heather Belle" from Cardiff was the first paddle steamer to use the pier, on 15 June 1867. In this picture a Bristol Channel paddle steamer is seen operating from Birnbeck Pier. The 1,040ft pier and toll-house were listed as an historic monument in 1974, five years before the last regular steamer sailing. During the Victorian and Edwardian times, there were entertainments on the pier as can be seen at the centre of this picture; these included a switchback, waterchute, bioscope theatre, banqueting hall, indoor roller skating rink, pavilion and refreshment room. During the 1903 storm both jetties were damaged and later the left-hand jetty was removed for good.

The Grand Pier: 'Arrived safe 10.20 am'. This postcard was sent from Weston to Park Street, Bristol at 1.15 pm 30th May 1905. Weston-super-Mare was often called "The Brighton of Bristol". The panorama depicted on this postcard was very popular with photographers and a similar view would have been seen by Weston's first settlers, firstly from the Iron Age encampment and later from the Roman hill fort. Note the stones from the early encampment in the foreground of the picture. Holy Trinity Church is in the centre of the picture. It was built in 1861, and a guidebook to the church likened the spire to a finger pointing to God and to Heaven: 'This is the purpose of the church – to this end it was built'. Now Elim Pentecostal Church, it is situated in Atlantic Road.

The second postcard is a slightly different view from the previous one of the pier, and dates prior to 1916. Note the extension to the pier, shown on this very rare postcard.

Weston has the second highest rise and fall of tide in the world and this, combined with strong sea currents caused problems to the mooring of steam ships. To overcome this, the Grand Pier was extended in 1905, to a total length of 2,580 feet. Despite the extension the Grand Pier proved not to be long enough for Pleasure Steam Ships to call in safely at all tides. In 1916, work began to dismantle the extension, except for the 40 yards beyond the Pavilion. The work was completed by the end of the First World War.

The 'New' Grand Pier, pictured on a contemporary postcard of 1904. The Pier's Manager during the 1920s was the greatly-liked and well-remembered Harry Broomfield who was beginning to make the pier a more successful concern, aided on the administrative side by Mr P.D. O'Connell.

On 13 January 1930, the Grand Pier caught fire. At this time there was a theatre on the pier situated in the pavilion with a balcony around it. Regular shows and live bands were a feature, dancing lessons were also held. Being built of wood, it burnt well and was soon burnt to the ground – or to the sea. Westonians at the time recorded how it could be seen burning from Milton Road.

The pier was sold after the fire and a new pavilion was built without a theatre. This re-opened in 1933 housing the amusements and funfair, that have been updated to this present day.

21 September 1905. Interior of the new pavilion on the Grand Pier, Weston-super-Mare

Glentworth Bay, Weston-super-Mare. Note the waves on the shore line. Glentworth Bay became known as the Marine Lake in 1928, when a causeway with a retaining wall and sluices were built to enclose the cove. The postcard reads 'We have passed miles and miles of mountains on our sea voyage', The date was July 1911 and steam paddle ships were very important to Weston, bringing in the holiday-makers. They landed at the Old Pier on Birnbeck Island.

The White Funnel and Red Funnel Fleets

P & A Campbell's White Funnel fleet offered pleasure trips to Steep Holm and Flat Holm, South Wales and towns along the Severn Estuary. Most of the Campbell fleet served in both world wars and finally finished their pleasure trips in the Bristol Channel in 1967. They were replaced by the Waverley Steam Navigation Company of Glasgow with their *Prince Ivanhoe*, *Waverley* and *Balmoral*.

Enc

P. & A. CAMPBELL Limited, Steamers.

'BRITANNIA,' 'CAMBRIA,' 'WESTWARD HO!' 'RAVENSWOOD,' 'WAVERLEY,'
'GLEN ROSA,' 'BONNIE DOON' 'BRIGHTON QUEEN,' 'ALBION,' &c.

TELEGRAPHIC ADDRESSES :	TELEPHONE NOS.	
"RAVENSWOOD, BRISTOL."	BRISTOL	3112
	CLEVEDON	17
"PRIMROSE, CARDIFF."	CARDIFF	211
	NEWPORT	0560
	MINEHEAD	4
"RODNEY HOUSE, NEWPORT"	WESTON-S-MARE	44
	LYNMOUTH	0196
"PIERMASTER, CLEVEDON."	ILFRACOMBE	37

1 Britannia Buildings, Cumberland Basin,
BRISTOL, November 4th 190 8

Secretary

Weston-super-Mare Hospital

Weston-super-Mare.

Dear Sir,

We have much pleasure in sending you the enclosed cheque £IO:IO:O ,being part proceeds of Charity Trip run by us on IOth of September last.

Yours faithfully,

P & A. CAMPBELL Ltd
Secretary.

From Ship to Shore, 1908. The proceeds from this charity trip went to the original Weston Hospital. As an aside – the General Hospital in the Boulevard incorporated the older hospital and was one of the last major buildings constructed from local stone. The Boulevard is known as 'Stone Street' because of its fine buildings.

RED FUNNEL STEAMERS.

Special Cheap Trip to

LYNMOUTH, ILFRACOMBE

AND CRUISE TO

Lundy Island

to view the Battleship " Montague,"

by the Gwalia,

SATURDAY, July 21st,

(Weather and Circumstances permitting).

Leave Weston, 9.10 a.m.   Returning from Ilfracombe, 3 p.m. ; Lynmouth, 3.35 p.m.

SPECIAL CHEAP RETURN FARES
Ilfracombe, 2/6.   Lundy, 3/6

EVENING TRIP TO NEWPORT.
Leave Weston, 5.40 p.m. Returning from Newport, 7.40 p.m.
RETURN FARE, ONE SHILLING.

Further particulars apply—
Telephone 88, Weston.   J. CHARLTON, Red Funnel Office, Pier Gates, Weston.

This original poster for a trip on the *Gwalia* is dated 21st July 1906. The ship, part of the Red Funnel fleet was then 17 months old when it sailed from Weston's Birnbeck Pier.

Gwalia Special Trip to view the stranded *HMS Montague* in 1906. The *HMS Montague* was a Duncan class battleship, launched in 1901 with a displacement of 14,000 tons and a crew of 750. She was the latest of her type to be built before the *Dreadnought*. No lives were lost when the *Montague* went aground in fog on the Shutters, Lundy Island – Wednesday 13 May 1906. Long and costly efforts to refloat her were to be to no avail, and she became a total wreck despite the use of four other battleships, a cruiser and several tugs. They all failed to free her from the rocks. *(Photograph supplied by F. Gibson)*

Gwalia: **the ship with three names**

There were three fleets of steamers which ran regular services between the Bristol Channel Ports – the Red, Yellow and White Funnel Fleets. Eventually, only P & A Campbell's White Funnel Fleet survived the fierce competition of the time. The *Gwalia* served in each of the three fleets during her eventful career at sea. She was built by J Brown & Co Ltd, of Clydebank and these were her vital statistics:

Gwalia	Beam 29 feet
G.R.T. 519 tons	Speed 20 knots
Length 245 feet	Displacement 700 tons

The two-funnel paddle steamer was launched on 24 February 1905, she was originally named *Gwalia* and was built for the Barry Railway Company who operated the Red Funnel Steamer Fleet. A worthy competitor to P & A Campbell's fleet, the Barry Railway Company was restricted to certain routes and ports and eventually their operations were no longer viable. The first trip of the *Gwalia* as a Red Funnel ship was made to Ilfracombe on 19 April 1905. She was one of the fastest and largest passenger ships operating in the Bristol Channel.

"Gwalia" (Picture supplied by Nigel Coombes)

The *Gwalia* was sold in 1910 to the Furness Railway Company, and renamed *Lady Moyra*. During World War I, *Lady Moyra* served as a mine-sweeper and after the war was sold to the Yellow Funnel Fleet of W Tucker of Cardiff, still in competition with Campbell's fleet.

In 1922, the ship was auctioned when the Yellow Funnel Fleet went out of business. Campbells bought her and she remained in the Bristol Channel. In 1932, *Lady Moyra* was re-registered at Bristol and renamed *The Brighton Queen*, becoming the largest of the White Funnel fleet. She was sent to the South Coast where she made regular trips to Boulogne and Calais. She stayed there until World War II broke out and was again converted at Milford Haven to a mine-sweeper. On 31 May 1940, when returning from the French port of Dunkirk with 700 troops on board, she was struck and sunk by German bombers. There was a heavy loss of life, although all the Bristol crew on board were rescued.

The headline in a newspaper report dated Saturday 8 June 1940 read "*Brighton Queen* Steamer sunk at Dunkirk". It went on to say: "A Pleasure steamer of Messrs P & A Campbell's famous Bristol Channel fleet played its part in the epic story of the evacuation of British, French and Belgian forces from Northern France whose position had been rendered untenable by the surrender of the Belgian King. Amid this was the loss of six destroyers and 24 minor losses, plus the sinking of the White Funnel vessel the "Brighton Queen". It has since been reported that the vessel played a heroic part in the rescue. The "Brighton Queen" went down under a rain of bombs after she had been called from mine sweeping to carry out rescue work and while assisting another vessel which had gone aground. She had previously got into the mole at Dunkirk and taken on board, under heavy bombardment, 600 Algerian and French troops. When she got out into the open sea the bombers concentrated upon her, and she was hit in the stern and foundered. Nearly all her officers and crew were saved.

The Waverley

1993 saw the recommencement of steamer trips and the return of both the *Balmoral* and the *Waverley*. They were not able to use Birnbeck Pier which was closed to the public and awaiting repairs. The Pier was the only place available for outbound and return trips with a sufficient depth of water until changes were made at Knightstone Island. This followed the introduction of docking facilities comprising four 'greenheart' timber bulks strapped to the sea walls and two additional mooring posts set in concrete on the island. Projecting rocks on the foreshore had their tops removed to provide sufficient depths for ships to dock. Depending on the tide times, the return journey can entail disembarking at Clevedon's historic pier and a coach trip back to Weston.

The registered charity which runs the *Balmoral* and the *Waverley* have kept alive the Victorian tradition of Pleasure Steamers sailing the Bristol Channel. It is interesting to note that the preservation society is based in Gwalia Buildings, Barry Docks – the building is named after the *Gwalia* Paddle Steamer.

The Waverley – the last seagoing paddle steamer in the world. The *Waverley* is pictured in 1986 docked at Narrow Quay, Bristol. The Arnolfini Arts Complex Building is behind. This building was featured on the 28p stamp issued on 10 April 1984, one of four stamps which drew attention to design and construction in the urban environment.

The Turning of Time. Here are the turnstiles at Weston's Birnbeck Pier pictured on 13 April 1993. They were used to control the crowds and to prevent people entering without paying. Many thousands have passed through these gates to pay for their tickets to board the paddle steamers from the fleets of a bygone age. On August Bank Holiday, 1892, an estimated 15,000 people met 8 waiting steamers; this was quite usual.

The only things landing on this jetty now are fish. Birnbeck Pier was closed to the public in 1993 and 1994, but the local fishing club still had access to fish from the end of the pier. Birnbeck Sea Angling Club founder members, John Mason pictured left, and Bob Keyes who is pictured right, the son of Robert featured elsewhere in this book, fish in all weathers on the Birnbeck Pier jetty. John is the Secretary of the Club, Bob is a past Chairman. The lifeboat still operates from the pier which, in 1995, remains closed to the public.

The Pleasure Steamer *Balmoral* 'registered for 800 passengers' called at Knightstone Harbour for the first time on Friday 23 July 1993. Westonians and holiday visitors boarded for a sea cruise to Ilfracombe. The *Balmoral* celebrated her 25th Anniversary of visits to the Bristol Channel that year. The Bristol based *Balmoral* was built in 1947 and joined the former White Funnel Fleet in the Bristol Channel and other areas in 1968. In 1980 the company went out of business and the ship was laid up in Avonmouth. She was later sold and became a floating pub in Dundee. When the pub business failed, the ship was rescued and returned following a refit in Glasgow and brought back into service in the Bristol Channel in 1986.

Trams and Trains

Horses and carriages were the only competition to the tram in the early years, and it took some time for horses to get used to the electric trams when they were first introduced. They ran on six miles of tramlines around the town and were very popular both with Westonians and holiday-makers.

April 1937 saw the ending of trams in Weston; increasing use of the motor car and competition from buses both played their part in their demise. Trams were slow and caused obstructions on the highway, although they were still very popular and were carrying up to 45,000 fare-paying passengers on a Bank Holiday shortly before they were withdrawn from service. They were later broken up at their Locking Road depot.

"Where could we get on the W.C. & P.?"

In years gone by, this was the ambiguous question many visitors asked as they arrived for their holidays at the seaside. The W.C. & P. was the Weston, Clevedon & Portishead light railway. The railway began operations between Clevedon and Weston in 1897 and ten years later the extension to Portishead was built. The cost of this put the W.C. & P. into receivership in 1909 and it stayed in debt until the line closed.

Seaside holidays and the countryside were a great attraction for visitors and locals alike. Holiday-makers who came from Wales on the paddle steamers could continue their journeys to Weston by rail, or visit nearby Clevedon or Portishead. In the first full year of working the W.C. & P. carried a quarter of a million passengers. The steam engines and diesel cars were kept and serviced at Clevedon, where a shopping centre occupies the site today.

May 1902 saw the introduction of trams to the streets of Weston. This post card is dated 27 July 1903; it was sent from Weston to Manchester. The streets are free of traffic as the tram pauses to let people disembark. The Grand Pier has not yet been built, as can be seen from the open view of Weston's beach.

The former Weston Terminus of the W.C. & P. is pictured here on 20 March 1993 in Ashcombe Road, Weston-super-Mare. The Terminus was three-quarters of a mile from the Weston sea front, so the light railway company ran a company horse bus. The round trip called at Ashcombe Road, High Street and the Pier. The building is now a pharmacist's shop. The path to the left of this shop was the end of the line for the W.C. & P.

The railway was slow and could not compete with the improving road transport, so it closed for good during the Second World War after a 43-year life span. The last train ran on Saturday 18 May 1940. The permanent way was no longer permanent toward the end of 1942: it was removed as scrap metal for the war effort.

High and Dry at Low Tide. The former W.C. & P. siding jetty on the Weston side of the River Yeo is showing its age in this picture but it has stood the test of time and is more than a memory, as can be seen. Small boats unloaded coal from South Wales into the waiting railway trucks. Engines were not able to use the jetty because of their weight. The trucks were taken on and off the jetty using a hawser attached to an engine or tractor. The jetty is constructed on a concrete platform supported on concrete and wooden piles. A single line was laid on it. The track sleeper grooves could still be seen in April 1993 when this picture was taken. There were Halts at Ebdon Lane and Wick St Lawrence. A low embankment carried the railway line on to the Wick St Lawrence Bridge over the River Yeo, and the former bridge was 240ft long. At the midway point of the bridge was the three mile marker from Clevedon.

These two pictures were taken from the middle of the pathway adjoining Chesham Road North, to the right of the top picture. Chesham Road South is to the right of the picture below. The cycle path gives a good idea of the former light railway route entering the Weston terminus at Ashcombe Road in the far distance of the top picture. The route leaving the Weston terminus can be seen in the lower picture. This view was soon to be lost shortly after these pictures were taken on 7 May 1994. The land was developed and houses were built on part of this open site, though there is still a cycle track.

Weston on The High Speed route

The first high speed passenger train service was on 5 May 1975 from Bristol Parkway to Paddington – a journey time of 1 hour 56 minutes. The following day, the train visited Weston while still on passenger trials. The passenger accommodation consisted of the latest design Mark III coach and set new standards in passenger environment. During its trials the train set a world speed record for diesel traction of 143 mph.

The author's early morning trip on the HST was while the train was still on passenger trials on 30 May 1975 from Weston to Bristol Temple Meads. The train was not announced in advance as being the HST, it was a case of being aware of the trials in the hope that it was in service at that time and on that date. A new era of speed and comfort began in 1976, 125mph trains were to become a regular feature.

From Track to the Future: The Return of Steam

During April and July 1985, Weston-super-Mare saw the return of Steam Passenger trains to BR track to coincide with the 150th Anniversary of the Great Western Railway.

On the 8 April 1985 Hagley Hall No 4930 and Hinton Manor No 7819 were coupled together and called at Weston General Station. They were making a water stop and two large waiting Dairy Crest Milk lorries piped water aboard the two steam trains. Large crowds lined the platforms and surrounding areas to view the scene – crowds were also waiting along the route to Bristol on bridges and by the side of the track. Weston Milton station platform was full of people with cameras, knowing the steam trains were not stopping but they all waited to capture the moment.

14 July 1985, Weston Station. Hagley Hall is being prepared to continue its journey to Bristol. Pictured here is Elizabeth, wife of Robert Keyes, featured elsewhere in this book.

Sun, Sand and Sea

The Pavilion on Knightstone Island – "I'm having a jolly time here. Weather beautiful" wrote the sender of this card in July 1906. Notice the open sea view before the sea wall and Marine Lake Pavilion were built, on the land in the foreground; the latter has since been pulled down. Inside the Marine Lake Pavilion there was a Sealife Aquarium and Mini Zoo, open front shops and public conveniences served the entrance to the Marine Lake.

The Two Bays, Weston-super-Mare. Madeira Cove is in the foreground. This postcard view of the two bays posted on 9 July 1907 sent by a servant girl who came to Weston to recover from illness. She came to enjoy the sea air and was writing to her employer to say all was well. Note the tram in the foreground; because of their appearance, the Weston summer trams had the popular nickname given to them of "toast racks". 'Air Like Wine' went the advertising slogan of the day. *The Westonian* guidebook of 1829 said "Not long since, a medical gentleman of celebrity, resident at Bath, sent 100 patients to Weston, for the benefit of the air, only 4 of whom left the place without being benefited."

Weston-super-Mare from the South. The Seafront scheme was completed in 1886, a new sea wall from Anchor Head to the Sanatorium. A few years later, horse and carriages drive along the sea front. Note the tram lines in the road. The Beach Lawns were opened in 1910; the Grand Pier work started in 1903 and it opened on 11 June 1904; the landing stage was added in 1905. Note the old Weston-super-Mare Coat of Arms.

Memories are made of this: the Marine Lake Pavilion as pictured on a stick of Weston Rock.

The Knightstone Pavilion Theatre was built in 1902 at the same time as the swimming baths, situated just behind the building. Accommodation was provided for an audience of 1,200 people.

There were live acts and films shown in the Theatre. After the First World War had ended it was used to hold a Thanksgiving Service in 1918.

Next to the theatre is the Marine Lake. Sea water from the Marine Lake used to be pumped to large settling tanks for use in the swimming baths a few yards away. The seawater was cleaned and the mud left to settle in the large tanks built onto the rock surface of the island. Access to these tanks was via a tunnel leading from an exit door behind the interior of the main swimming baths; a maintenance tunnel crossed under the road to beneath the theatre's foundations. The tunnel was small and dark and one needed a torch to light the way. Once there, the large man-made tanks, seeming as large as lakes, could be viewed as well as the surface rock on which the buildings had been constructed. The tanks were still in use until the 1960s, pumping seawater into the swimming baths.

A knight's statue kept watch above the baths. Knightstone Island is said to have derived its name from having been the burial place of a Roman knight, who probably had been stationed either at their settlement at Uphill, or at their camp above on the summit of Worle Hill Knightstone Swimming Baths was opened on 13 May 1902 by the Deputy Lieutenant of Somerset, Mr J.J. Jackson Barstow, of Weston-super-Mare.

Weston-super-Mare was one of fifteen towns chosen to take part in the European Heritage Days which was an international event. The two days chosen were 11 and 12 September 1993. Among the buildings open for public viewing in the town were the former Knightstone Swimming Baths and Doctor Fox's 1822 bath house next door.

The Knightstone Theatre still stands. This picture was taken from the centre of the stage. The first floor balcony reminds us of a bygone era when it was a hive of entertainment. The theatre closed for several years and its future is undecided, with plans for renewal of the building and a change of use.

A balcony view of the six-lane Knightstone indoor pool looking from the deep end six feet six inches to the shallow end three feet three inches. The pool was one hundred feet long by thirty five feet wide. When built there were two 'pools' one reserved for the ladies, later to be made into a children's pool and the large men's baths, which later became the general pool. The changing cubicles were beneath the balcony before modernisation. This picture was taken on 28 March 1992 at 3.45 pm. A few days later the swimming baths closed.

The Knightstone Swimming Baths, 11 September 1993. Empty of people and water, the Knightstone swimming baths as seen from the two metre deep mark. Do you remember resting your feet on the water inlet pipe to the bottom left of the photograph?

The fine oval staircase inside the hallway of Doctor Fox's bath house. This listed building had been boarded up awaiting redevelopment of Knightstone Island. The former hot and cold baths described in 1824 as "Plunging and shower baths of sea water, each bath having a private dressing room attached to it".

"Oh I do like to be beside the seaside, I do like to be beside the sea" – Weston's Marine Lake, 1962. The lake was and still is a safe cove for family fun and games, or just relaxing in the sunshine. The covered walkway was removed following the 1981 storm damage, as was the former model railway building to the right of the picture. Above the model railway entrance, there was a large cut-out picture depicting a steam train speeding out of a tunnel. The model railway was a former favourite for the young and older person alike. People often took a welcome break from the sunshine or showers to view the many model trains speeding through tunnels in landscape scenes. The centre always looked much bigger inside than its outside appearance. The model railway layout was later housed at the Tropicana building on Weston's sea front.

The Fury of the Sea

Weston-super-Mare suffered considerable damage to its sea front during the storm of the night of 13th December 1981. High winds and a pounding sea broke up the tarmac surface on the Promenade. The town had not seen storm damage on a similar scale since the great storm of 1903 which resulted in part of the Knightstone Causeway collapsing into the sea.

There was an air of excitement in watching the power of the sea, as the water crashed against the shore. The sea spray stung the faces of people nearby, a timely reminder not to take nature and the elements for granted.

As a result of the storm, the Rozel Music Gardens were later demolished in March 1983; today, there is an enclosed modern shelter known as the Rozel shelter and cafe. After the storm, the Promenade decks surrounding Madeira Cove and the Marine Lake were pulled down. The Marine Lake walkway had collapsed into the sea; when the covered walk was cleared, the area returned to its Victorian appearance, with the natural looking stone sea wall. The Marine Lake was drained of water while the storm clearance work was undertaken in 1981. During this time the Model Railway Hall was pulled down; this was formerly the Cove Pavilion where a Pierrot concert party performed. The Marine Lake Pavilion was later levelled as part of the sea front improvement programme during 1987.

The Marine Lake was opened in 1928. The lake was formed by the building of a breakwater, completed in 1929, with an approximate length of 350 yds across Glentworth Bay. The sea can be regulated to let the sea water in and out and it encloses about 9 acres of water.

After the storm:, 1pm on 14th December – Lucille Christopher on her way to Weston College pauses to view the sea wall coping stones laid tossed to one side despite their weight.

Storm damage at the Madeira Cove/Marine Lake, photographed at 1.10 pm on 14 December 1981.

Historic Weston Buildings – some long since gone

The southerly aspect of La Retraite School, South Road, with views over Weston Bay. On Wednesday 10 November 1971, at 3.00 pm there was a Sale by Auction of La Retraite School, South Road, Weston-super-Mare. It was soon to become a victim of redevelopment – the building was demolished and, called Rainham Court, took its place in 1981. During the Second World War the school library was used as a convalescent ward for our soldiers recovering from their injuries, nursed by the Red Cross. Although the use of the classrooms may have changed over the years the main rooms used were as follows: Basement level: Art Room. Ground floor: front left corner, Library. Ground floor front middle rooms, all classrooms. Ground floor front right corner: Music room. First floor top right: 5th and 6th form class rooms. Top floor left, nuns' extra living quarters. The adjoining building behind to the right had a top floor science room, and on the ground floor was the school gym.

The Grand Atlantic Hotel and town bus station. This picture was taken from the former footbridge spanning the sea front. The hotel was originally built as a school in 1854, becoming a hotel in 1889. It is set in 6 acres of grounds with 120 rooms, a large reception, reading rooms, smoke room, billiard room and oriental lounge. In this 1987 picture, the hotel stands tall beside the town's only bus station, now demolished. The buses went into the station through the right entrance and departed through the left entrance. The grey painted house to the left adjoining the former bus station was also cleared to make way for apartments, Carlton Mansions, alongside the Grand Atlantic Hotel.

All change: the town's former bus station clock is now sited on the beach lawns. In the background is the site of the former Salisbury Terrace replaced by the Sovereign Shopping Centre which opened on 7 April 1992.

1988: The Salisbury Hotel. A last look before the bulldozers came in. Salisbury Terrace is situated beside the Winter Gardens; Boarded up and now unsafe, it was awaiting demolition.

The former Salisbury Hotel was at one time owned by Avon County Council and operated by the Social Services Committee. It was bought by Bristol City Council in 1973 for £180,000. Avon took it over in 1974 when the county was created. Avon Council sold it for £290,000 in 1980. Bristol Council used the hotel to provide holidays for needy people and it was only partly run on a commercial basis. It was sold because Avon decided at the end of 1979 to take economy measures due to the decreasing number of Social Services clients using the hotel.

It also catered for tourist and business visitors and in the 1970s had 56 bedrooms. The Avon Suite seated 135 at tables, 200 in rows, and room for 200 to dance. The Windsor Room seated 30 and was suitable for small

Three, Two, One: In July 1993, another major redevelopment was considered by Woodspring District Council, West Area committee. The Area in question was in Weston's main shopping street. The empty Golden Spur restaurant and the former Youngsters toy shop next door were the two shops to be demolished. This picture was taken on a busy Saturday in Weston's High Street, on 3 July 1993. Permission was applied for the three-storey buildings housing the two shops to be demolished and replaced with one big shop. The two shops are situated in the centre of this picture, with the large twin adjoining arched windows above the shops.

As seen in 1995: the former Youngsters toy shop and the Golden Spur cafe were demolished to make way for a new two-storey building in Weston's High Street.

The Winter Gardens

On 14 July 1927 the Winter Gardens and Pavilion were officially opened by Ernest Palmer, deputy chairman of the Great Western Railway. This ceremony was preceded by one at which T.E. MacFarlane, Chairman of the Council, opened the gate in Post Office Road with a golden key. That gateway minus the gates could still be seen in the next picture taken in 1987. In 1989 the Winter Gardens were closed for complete refurbishment and extension into the new Town Square Gardens.

Post Office Road, leading to the Winter Gardens and Pavilion. This area was also to be redeveloped around the Winter Gardens and new shopping centre. Compare the diifferent style of the telephone kiosk in this picture with that on page 45.

Royal Arcade, 1987. The rows of small shops are closed up, awaiting demolition. This view is towards Post Office Road. The Royal Arcade and Post Office Road became the Sovereign Centre.

Post Office Road, Weston. The entrance to Royal Arcade was beneath the Cecil Walker sign in 1987. This clothes shop still trades today. The Royal Arcade became a part of the Sovereign Centre. The main Post Office building was to the right, and the First and Second Class posting boxes fitting into the wall of the building behind the people in the picture are bottom right.

The Winter Gardens in 1988 before they were redesigned in 1992 when the shopping centre was built. The rear of the Post Office building can be seen and the area where the Post Office delivery vans used to park on the other side of the High Wall.

The new design of the Winter Gardens was planned for the twenty-first century. The old building was restored and upgraded, the tennis courts were demolished and a new conference complex built in their place. Her Royal Highness The Princess Royal opened the new look Winter Gardens on 21 January 1992. The area around the Winter Gardens was also redeveloped.

Post Office Road, 1987. Off the High Street, at the rear of the Winter Garden Pavilion, stood Weston's main Post Office. This was on the site of the Sovereign Centre. Directly in front of the white van is Youngster's Toy Shop and the Golden Spur restaurant; to the right of the van is the National Westminster bank and Cecil Walker's clothes shop.

The Italian Gardens

The New Promenade, Weston-super-Mare. The Italian Gardens alongside the main High Street in Weston – the postcard is dated 15 August 1929. The town map of 1931 showed that the buildings in South Parade viewed from the High Street left to right were Westminster Bank Limited, Imperial Hotel, the Weston-super-Mare Club, Liverpool Victoria Friendly Society, E.T. Gillmore Architect, Pedrick & Morgan Auctioneers, and Lloyds Bank Limited.

The Italian Gardens improvement scheme.

The Sovereign Centre and the newly-created Town Square Gardens are the backdrop to the changing face of Weston in October 1992. The stonework along the length of the Italian Gardens was presented to Weston by Henry Butt JP,CC in June 1924, the event being recorded by a plate on the wall.

A clipped hedge had been planned to separate the Italian Gardens from the former putting green. By chance, Harry Brown, the town's Surveyor, knew of a fine Portland Stone terrace with statuary representing the four seasons .It was probably brought from Italy, but was for sale at the old home of Alexander Brudges at Beddington House, Croydon. The house had been requisitioned during the First World War and this stonework was the perfect answer to screen the High Street, and Henry Butt provided the purchase money.

Glentworth Hall

Glentworth Hall, Knightstone Road, Weston-super-Mare (picture Woodspring Central Library). The hall was built in 1853/4 and demolished in June 1973. It was among the first half-dozen gentlemen's residences to be built in the resort. Richard Parsley and William Cox were the first two men to start a building development at Weston in the early years of the last century. Cox partnered Parsley in building Weston's first hotel, Reeves, later called Rogers and now the Royal Hotel. John Cox built Glentworth Hall as his own residence. It was much admired in former days but it was later not deemed of sufficient architectural interest (!) to be listed for preservation. Only the front entrance path porch remains of the original Glentworth Hall. People started to become aware of Weston's heritage when in 1973 Glentworth Hall was demolished and Glentworth Court, multi-storey flats, took its place on the Weston skyline.

Hospitals

Weston General Hospital: all closed up and out of commission following the opening of Weston's new General Hospital in 1986. Originally known as the Queen Alexandra Memorial Hospital, it was opened 6th July 1928 by the Duke and Duchess of York who were later to become King George VI and Queen Elizabeth. This picture shows the former public front door entrance adjoining the Boulevard.

Above the Boulevard entrance to the former hospital was the main operating theatre, pictured here long after the hospital had closed.

Situated in the outside front stone walls of the old General Hospital were three historic memorial stones: The first was laid on the 11th November 1926 by Walter Farrer, Archdeacon of Wells and Provincial Grand Master of Somerset. The second was laid by Ernest E Baker, who was the resort's first historian, and among those who each contributed £1,000 toward the cost of building of Weston's Memorial Hospital. As well as holding the position of Honorary Secretary of the hospital for 25 years, he occupied the presidential chair for three terms: 1903-05, 1910-12 and 1921-23. One of the wards in the hospital was named after him. He made his home at Glebe House, formerly The Rectory, which is Weston's oldest residence. As well as his work as a solicitor, he was a director of Birnbeck Pier Company. A man who did a lot for the town, his

40 year association with the hospital was unbroken at the time of his death aged 76 on 27 March 1931. The third stone was laid by Henry Butt Esq JP.CC President 11 November 1926.

Either side of the main entrance double doors, carved into the stone work of the building was the date 1927. One year later the hospital had the official opening and naming ceremony.

A large free standing stone memorial in front of and opposite the hospital doors situated in the low boundary wall with adjoining ornamental railings either side, commemorated the 1928 opening.

May 1994: The Old Weston General Hospital Chapel/Mortuary had been surrounded by foliage. The building within was in a state of ruin, with the exception of the rear stained glass window. During November 1994 work started on the new housing development. The buildings on the site behind the derelict main hospital building including this chapel were demolished. The hospital site was then set to be redeveloped in a £3 million scheme to provide more than 50 new homes. The front entrance to the hospital on The Boulevard was to be developed into 16 new flats and to be named Henry Butt House.

The rear stained glass window

The new hospital at Weston, opened on 16th September 1986. This is from a commemorative card issued by the League of Friends

The writing was on the wall on 23rd August 1986: "This Hospital is now closed. All maternity services are being provided by the General Hospital".

Ashcombe House

During the First World War Ashcombe House, which was well-situated at the top end of a cul-de-sac called The Drive, was used as a base and hospital by the Red Cross for wounded soldiers. On 14 January 1918 there was a severe fire which damaged the house. It was thought that a chimney overheated. After the war, the building was used by Somerset County Council as offices and later made into flats. It suffered bomb damage during the Second World War and was left empty until the Duchess of Kent opened it in June 1946 as the local Maternity Hospital.

The stone shown here was once part of the former maternity hospital. It was salvaged after the house was demolished and the site cleared in 1986. The stone was situated inside the front entrance hallway of the house, and formed the right-hand side of the wall, beside the front door. The frame of the front door was fitted into the left-hand side of this stone. The round bell push space can be seen under the writing at the foot of the stone — familiar to generations of expectant mothers and anxious fathers. During April 1993, redevelopment work started with the building of seven four-bedroomed houses.

The Royal West of England Sanatorium

Pictured 6 March 1993, 125 years after being built, the former Royal Hospital on the south end of Weston's sea front, was waiting for a new lease of life having been shut for six years following the opening of the town's £20 million general hospital. Many convalescents have come here through the years to recover since the hospital was built in 1868. The buildings on the 2.8 acre site were a testimony to the salubrity of Weston's sea air and its health-giving benefits to the sick. Queen Victoria commanded the institution should enjoy the prefix "Royal".

The old hospital had planning consent to convert the buildings into luxury residential flats. The listed chapel, to the far left of the picture, was to be brought back into use as a private place of worship for the flat owners, if future conversion were to take place. As the Royal hospital expanded over the years additional buildings were built in the rear grounds of the main hospital site of 1868.

Weston High Street: a post card posted at 7.30 pm on 15 January 1914. Note the townsfolk all looking toward the cameraman. The shops from left to right are: Lance & Lance Limited of Waterloo House – they were drapers and furnishers until the 28/29 June 1942 World War II bombing; next door, Davies Bros, was a stationer's shop which sold Swan inks and fountain pens and was a bookseller and printer. The next building was Georges Limited who were cooks and confectioners, the Belle Vue restaurant was also in the building.

The Way We Were: Weston-super-Mare open air swimming pool, measuring 220 feet by 140 feet. The diving board stage which was 33 feet high had seven stages. The pool had a deep end of 15 feet, a spring board and two water slides. Situated on the beach opposite Clevedon Road, it was opened in 1937 and cost over £50,000. It held 850,000 gallons of filtered and chlorinated sea water. The pool when full held 1,500 bathers who could use the sunbathing enclosures and sun-lounge cafe, it also had an artificial beach. Today it is the Tropicana fun pool. (Picture: Woodspring Central Library).

Clarence Park. Weston - Super-Mare.

Clarence Park. This postcard was postmarked 4.30 pm 10 September 1905, and was sent to Tewkesbury. Clarence Park was a popular park in Weston with its trees, fountain and flower beds, shelters and seats. The park is still popular to this day. It covers sixteen acres and was presented to the town by Rebecca Davies, in memory of her late husband Henry Davies, October 1882. Henry Davies was the resort's greatest building speculator. He built Royal Crescent, Ellenborough Crescent, Manilla Crescent, Claremont Crescent and Oriel Terrace. Clarence Park was named after the Duke of Clarence, the brother of King George V. Originally the land donated was in a large field and was only later divided into two sections by Walliscote Road.

The fountain has remained unchanged to this day. It was presented to Weston-super-Mare by Spencer Tyler, Chairman of the town commissioners in memory of Rebecca Davies August 1883. Clarence Park was divided into two parks, known as East and West parks, the East Park is the home for the Weston county cricket festival. Somerset Cricket Club's annual festival was first held in 1914. There is also a cast-iron Coalbrookdale fountain on the Beach Lawns; this was donated to the town in 1910 by Thomas Macfarlane, whose family built the Grand Central Hotel. The features the figure of a cherub wrestling with a snake, a reference to the legend of Laocoan. In 1995, it was listed as a structure of special architectural and historic interest.

Weston's Golden Sands: 13 February 1993, home of the Weston Donkeys. Horse and cart rides have always been very popular. The donkeys have been a part of Weston since the early 1890s. When the Victorians turned the town into a seaside resort donkeys gave rides on the beach for the children. Before Weston became a holiday resort, donkeys were used to bring in the nets from the boats, when the town was no more than a small fishing port. In earlier days there were 12 donkey pitches along Weston's sun-kissed sands, the owners taking turns for the best trading spot situated close to the Grand Pier. At the time of writing, only two owners keep donkey pitches, Don Trapnell and his cousin, Ron Mager. Flower Drew, Don's grandmother was a well-known personality on Weston beach keeping donkeys in the past days of fierce competition. Up to 150 donkeys were on the beach at any one time at a shilling a ride – today, a ride costs 50p.

Weston at War

"This morning, the British Ambassador in Berlin handed the German Government a final note stating that, unless we heard by 11 o'clock that they were prepared at once to withdraw their troops from Poland, a state of war would exist between us. I have to tell you that no such undertaking has been received, and that consequently this country is at war with Germany." – Radio broadcast by British Prime Minister Neville Chamberlain at 11am on September 3, 1939.

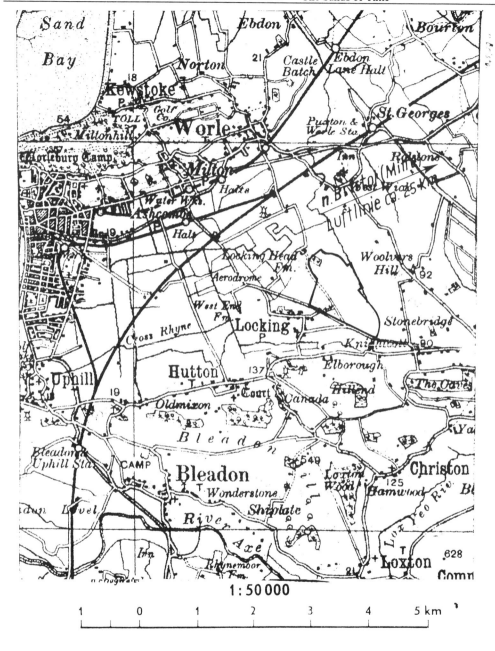

Targetting Weston-super-Mare.
This is one of the actual German maps used for the blitz on Weston in 1942 by the Germans. It is kept at Weston's reference library.

The German bomber aircraft lined themselves up for raids on the town centre by flying into Weston over the Grand Pier which pointed to the heart of the town, they then headed in a straight line toward Milton and returned back to the town centre to inflict their damage.

The Luftwaffe used twin-engine planes such as the Heinkel He-III and the Dornier Do-17. Damage was caused by high explosive and incendiary bombs. Pictured is a Heinkel He-III that flew over Britain during the War.

circling the town, then the ground trembled as bombs were dropped, one landed where we used to live in Arundell Road.

"I got the children out of the house and together with our next door neighbour we all went for cover in the alleyway, we laid on the floor, the planes were right above us.

"The Boulevard Congregational Church, the next building to us on the left was a direct hit. As incendiary bombs fell around us together with the high explosive bombs we looked toward the house. It had filled with thick grey smoke – an incendiary bomb had fallen straight down the chimney. We later returned to the house to open all the doors and windows but it did little use. We called the RAF chaps down from the hill to put the thing out. They told us that the chimney had stopped it going off and put the fire out.

'Britain Can Take It!' The RAF answer was a four-engined heavy bomber, the Avro Lancaster, which was ready for combat for the first time in March 1942 and was the mainstay of the night offensive on Germany. Pictured is a Lancaster with its response to 'Reichsmarshall' Hermann Goering commander of the Luftwaffe.

1 Longton Grove Road, June 1942

Mrs Nora O'Connell, aged 93, recalled on 16 February 1993 the events in the early hours of June 1942 when she heard the rumble of German bomber planes pass over her home.

"We heard them coming and we thought that they were *en route* to bomb Bristol which meant that they would be returning via Weston on their way back to Germany.

"My husband was in charge of his section of the Home Guard and was in Ashcombe Road which meant we had to face the danger separated in different parts of the town. I had six children and myself in the house, we heard the planes coming back

"We were lucky we did not get a scratch, but there were those that were not, and we must not forget them. We did not expect to be bombed two nights in a row in the same place, Lance's Corner on the High Street where Argos stands today was levelled to the ground as were other parts of the street in the Boulevard, bombs fell behind us in Grove Park as well. We often wondered why they bombed Weston, we can only guess the reasons."

On June 28-29 1942, the first bombs of that night were dropped just before the siren warnings at 0122 hours. On the second night, sirens at 0150 gave half an hour's warning before the attack.

The O'Connell family pictured in 1938 in what was 26 Arundell Road, Weston, shortly before moving to Longton Grove Road. Mrs O'Connell lived at 1 Longton Grove Road until 1978, and the house was made into flats in 1979. Left to right – Sheila, Brenda, Nora, Hugh, Patricia, and Maureen, Carmel was born the following year, the picture was taken by Mr O'Connell. Note: 26 Arundell Road was called "Manresa" and has since been renumbered to 44 Arundell Road.

The Night of the Air Raids on Weston

Mr and Mrs O'Connell had one son and five daughters. This account is recalled by one of their daughters, the second eldest, who was aged 14 at the time of the raid. The account was recalled in March 1993 when she was aged 64.

"I still have quite vivid memories of the Air Raids, in the early hours of 28 and 29 June 1942. When the siren sounded the alert, we ran downstairs grabbing our clothes and gathered in the dining room. We soon realised it was a really bad raid – bombs seemed to be dropping and exploding all around us. My father was out in the road, but the rest of the family crawled into our shelter – a "Morrisson", built like a table with an iron (or steel) top and thick wire-mesh sides, and it somehow made us feel safer, though a direct hit on the house by a high-explosive bomb would have sent us all to Kingdom Come, Morrisson shelter or not.

"It was the night before my little brother's sixth birthday – his presents were waiting for him on top of the "table" we were huddled under. He was terrified, and began to cry and scream. My youngest sister, Carmel, aged three, was more stout-hearted. "Don't worry Hughie", she said in a very comfortable voice, "Jesus is with us". I remember those words to this day, fifty one years on! They were true! We began to sing hymns and songs to drown out the terrifying sounds of the raid. My father came in frequently to see that we were all right... When some ex-

In 1942, Father Christmas was not the only person to look down the chimney of 1 Longton Grove Road that year, the home of Mr and Mrs P.D. O'Connell and their six children. The Germans had ideas of their own on that clear June night. The chimney can be seen in this picture taken in 1993. In the foreground is the alleyway where Mrs O'Connell and her children took shelter. The bombs and machine gun fire fell all around them. To the rear of the picture is the Boulevard United Reformed Church, known as Boulevard Congregational Church in 1942. It was built in 1876, on 28 June 1942 it was set alight as incendiary bombs rained down.

plosions seemed very near he would say those were our guns opening up – that was quite comforting, too – I think one of the most frightening memories of that night is of the sinister throbbing of the engines of the German bombers, as they drew nearer and nearer.

"Then an incendiary bomb fell on the house. My father dashed in and ushered us all out – we grabbed anything we could – I remember my mother clutching the clock – and ran out into the road. A few yards from our house was an archway between two houses, and we huddled there against one of the walls. Either a machine-gun bullet or a piece of shrapnel flew through the archway and hit the wall opposite us. It was wonderful to see a very strong stout young Airman who was billeted up the road dashing past and into our house with a stirrup-pump, to help to put out our fire. Very soon we were taken in by neighbours who lived across the road opposite our house, and we spent the rest of that terrifying night there.

"The next few weeks we spent with kind friends at Bleadon and I seem to remember that the weather was wonderful. The lady of the house said the children could eat all the strawberries they could find in the garden. She had a shock when she saw the inroads they had made into her raspberries which were just coming into luscious ripeness – the strawberries were few, and the raspberries looked very similar ..."

In 1939, Mr O'Connell became the Joint Founder of NO290 (Weston-super-Mare) Squadron Air Training Corps. He raised the Home Guard transport section, and later he commanded H Q Company and "D" Company of the 8th (Weston) Battalion Home Guard. Mr and Mrs O'Connell celebrated their golden wedding in May 1975. When Mrs O'Connell died aged 94, a Requiem Mass was celebrated by the Bishop of Clifton, the Rt Rev Mervyn Alexander, Canon Ryan and four parish priests. It was shared by a full congregation of family and friends.

R.B.1
16

MINISTRY OF FOOD
1953-1954

SERIAL NO.   **1**

M of F

BN 813765

RATION BOOK

Surname *O'CONNELL (NORA Initials)*

Address ....

IF FOUND RETURN TO ANY FOOD OFFICE

F.O. CODE No.

SW - C
2

Pictured is Mrs Nora O'Connell's 1953 – 1954 ration book, used by her at David Greig Limited, 36 Orchard Street, Weston-super-Mare and Howells Stores, 60 Orchard Street, Weston-super-Mare.

"Food Does not grow in the shops you know."

During the war years, food and other items were in short supply. As a result, food rationing was introduced for every person on Sunday, January 8, 1940. Butter, sugar and bacon were the first items controlled. Two months later on March 11 meat was added to the list. Unlike the earlier foodstuffs it was rationed by price rather than weight. The cheaper the cut, the more you got. Eggs were rationed in 1941.

Boulevard Congregational Church. The old Congregation Hall was used as a studio by the BBC from January 1941 until the 1942 June air raid

chapel was built in York Street, behind the Grand Central Hotel. The chapel soon proved too small, as at one time 10 per cent of Weston's population worshipped there, three years later in 1830 Church number two was built in High Street. It was a barn-like structure so a new church was built in 1858. It cost £2,300. Parts of the school-room can still be seen in the present day Wool-worth's store which now occupies the site. The congregation flourished as Weston started to grow and the time came to move again.

Church number four was built in the Boule-vard in 1876 in what was then a field, at a cost of £8,000. The population was 10,000. German bombs put an end to this church in 1942. Church number five stands today proudly in the Boule-vard with a large cross set in the east wall for all to see, walking or driving up the Boulevard.

Boulevard Congregational Church

The Rev H. Bickley was out on duty as an Air Raid Warden during the first hours of that morning when news reached him that his church had been hit by the German air raids. Although the church was destroyed by enemy action during World War II it was to rise again from the ashes. The opening of the rebuilt church was almost exactly 17 years later – it re-opened on 27 June 1959. The original stone was laid in August 1875; it was still intact and was incorpo-rated in the new church building. Local children used to play on the church site which became a haven for local cats during the 17 years the site remained an empty shell. Rev Bickley spent 12 years at the Boulevard Church. In the years that followed the bombing raid he kept his congregation together in borrowed buildings and then for many years in the old Boulevard Methodist Church.

One Church – Five Different Buildings

Congregationalism in Weston dated from about 1824 when the population of the town was 1,300. Members gathered in cottages for devotional services. The first church dated from 1827 when a

Boulevard Congregational Church.

RECONSTRUCTION
BAZAAR

ADMISSION BY PROGRAMME
6d.

TOWN HALL
Weston-super-Mare
THURSDAY,
DEC. 12th, 1946
10.30 a.m. to 7.30 p.m.

Lance & Lance, on the corner of Weston's High Street in 1935 (picture: Woodspring Central Library). On duty in Weston's High Street in 1935 was this RAC Scout directing the No 40 bus to Worle. The hand days of the scout were to end with the introduction of the new "robot signals" that were due to be shortly installed. The scout was soon to disappear, as was Lances' Corner seven years later.

Lance & Lance, June 1942. Shell-shocked from the air raid (picture by Bristol United Press). Note the traffic light to the right of the picture which remains intact, other street signs on Lances Corner had their tops blown off as a result of the bombing. The roads were on fire! The wooden blocks that had the appearance of small bricks or cobbles when they were laid down to make up the road surface caught alight in places around the town during the bombing raids.

The Shifting Sands of Time

Weston had good all-round visibility of the surrounding Bristol Channel coast line during World War II with views of open sea and the Welsh coast.

Birnbeck Pier was closed to the public between 1941-46, although it did not suffer the usual wartime fate of having a section cut out of it, since the pier was of a continuous girder construction. The admiralty took control of the pier during the war years. It was known as *HMS Birnbeck* and became a base for development of secret weapons. One can but hope that this fine Victorian pier remains standing as a continuous girder construction well into the next century.

Major repair works to the pier were still awaited during 1995. The thoughts at the time were that the sea would claim the structure if it remained closed to the public for a further length of time without works being done. The sands of time were taking their toll.

A Second World War Pillbox on the beach at Sand Bay Weston-super-Mare. Other examples can be seen around the Weston Airport area and others are at the end of Moor Lane, Hutton, on either side of the path.

A Pillbox on top of the dunes at Sand Bay. Shown in this photograph is Robert Spurling, the son of Robert Spurling Snr who owned the former Model Village on the seafront.

In The Line of Fire: German shell holes from the 1942 air raid remained in this wall at the top of Victoria Quadrant overlooking Longton Grove Road. Shortly after this photograph was taken in 1993, the wall was completely rebuilt because weathering had made it unsafe and the stonework was reused to rebuild the wall. A German aircraft cannon shell passed clean through the other stone, shown on the next page. These two stones were lying in the general pile of stonework awaiting relaying and no doubt would have been lost for all time in the newly rebuilt wall had they not been salvaged by the author. Carmel Keyes was 3 years old in 1942 and is pictured in March 1993; she is the youngest of Mr & Mrs O'Connell's six children.

The nights of terror: 28 and 29 June 1942

"Hitler knows that he will have to break us in this island or lose the war" – *Winston Churchill, British Prime Minister.*

During the forty-minute attack on these dates, Weston was bombarded with incendiaries and the streets were sprayed with cannon and machine gun bullets. There were 102 people killed and another 400 injured. It was a night of brilliant moonlight when Hitler's bombers came to town, a savage and deliberate attempt to hit Weston. It was estimated that 10,000 incendiary bombs fell in the two raids.

Grove Park, January 1941

A tree in Grove Park looks like any other mature tree, until you look more closely. There are metal railings impacted high up into the trunk of the tree, giving an effect of metal branches formed in a radial impact following the air raid on Weston by German bombers. The German high explosive bomb fell outside Grove Park shortly before 10.00 pm on 4 January 1941. This demolished the Grove Park Pavilion and did over £4,000 of damage to the Wadham Street Baptist Church, which only a short time before had had £1,700 spent on it and the work had only just been finished. Incendiary bombs added to the chaos which claimed many human victims. During the dusk-to-dawn raid, 34 people were killed within the Borough area, and some of the 85 injured later died. It was estimated that over 3,000 incendiary bombs fell on Weston that night as well as between 20 to 30 high explosives.

Mr A.T. Jones, caretaker of the Wadham Street Baptist Church, was at home with his wife and children. They had a very lucky escape during the air raid. They were all in the church house on the corner beside the church, and the house collapsed around them. Mr Jones managed to get out and raise help while his family took shelter under a table. It was 7.00 am the next morning before the "All Clear" was sounded. The Wadham Street Baptist Church and the hall were later razed to the ground during the June 1942 German air raid with only the church front façade left standing.

The author's exhibiton at Weston's Heritage Centre marking the 50th anniversary of VE Day on 8th May 1995. It included these stones that were damaged in a World War II air raid.

14 October 1940, 2119 hours — During the third siren of the evening, a stick of 12 bombs was dropped across Weston from the eastern to the northern boundary. A reservoir in Ashcombe Park was damaged, as well as many houses including one in Leewood Road. The main waterworks pumping plant escaped damage by a few yards. Robert Keyes was a Special Police Officer in Weston, during World War II. He was on duty during this time at Ashcombe Park on his bicycle when the bombs fell, and he had a lucky escape. He had a large patch to cover during the war years and came face to face with the German raiders whose aircraft had crashed. Robert carried out his police duties with great courage.

Hundreds of volunteers, wardens, ambulance workers, spe-

The Winter Gardens was a popular backdrop for local portrait photographers Crown Studios (formally of Arcade Corner, 23 Regent Street, Weston-super-Mare) as can be seen here in this 1928 picture of Elizabeth and Robert Keyes (1907 – 1991 & 1898 – 1972). They married in 1929, having met at the Grand Atlantic Hotel. His wartime exploits are described alongside.

cial constables, firemen, Home Guard, fire guards and others trained themselves to be of service not only in air raids but under invasion conditions. The Nazis could well have had designs on the Somerset coast, hoping to capture Bristol and cut communication to the South and North nearest to the sea.

During the World War II air raids over Weston, the Nazis totally destroyed 283 of the town's buildings, out of 8,447 affected, and including 581 offices and shops and 85 churches and public buildings. War damage repairs cost Weston Corporation £400,000. 1995 commemorates the 50th Anniversary of the ending of World War II.

The Spitfire

The symbol of the nation's courage, the Spitfire holds an enduring place in the heart of the nation. A symbol of defiance and hope for Britain during World War II.

From the dark days of 1940 to the victory in the air during the battle of Britain. The Spitfire's Rolls Royce Merlin engine was the latest in a series of engines to be named after birds of prey. It had been developed during the war with a two-stage 'blower' that gave it more power, and it was able to compete throughout the war with any other aircraft in the sky.

"Let Weston's aim be two Spitfires not one" exclaimed an excited local patriot. "We're only just in time about this as Watchet is collecting for a brace of battleships."

During both World Wars some aircraft were paid for by public subscriptions and private benefactors. These 'presentation' aircraft were often given names. Weston had a Spitfire paid for as a result of the town's efforts. The Spitfire II had the town's name painted on the side of the plane, RAF No P7925. "Weston-super-Mare" P7925 was one of the first MK II variants and was built at the Castle Bromwich factory. Every aircraft in the RAF had a card – Air Ministry Form 78 – known as Aircraft Movement cards, recording the units to which that aeroplane was allocated and noting when it was damaged and repaired. The aircraft were built as MK IIA/IIB/VA/VB between June 1940 and July 1941 by Vickers-Armstrong (Castle Bromwich) Limited, Birmingham. Contract no B981687/39/C23/(c). Serial range P7280 TO 8799.

Grove Park, "Victory Sunday", 13 May 1945 – Weston-super-Mare's 103rd Anniversary day. Major P.D. O'Connell is centre right of the bandstand centre pillar. He served with the 2/5 Norfolk Regiment 1915-19 and the 1st Bn Herts Regiment in France and Belgium during the First World War. This picture was taken for the Weston Gazette, the newspaper founded by Joseph Whereat. It was published for 106 years until 1951 when the title was bought by the 'Mercury' proprietors.

Major P.D. O'Connell was also involved in the Weston D-Day Appeal in 1944, Salute the Soldier Week also in 1944, and the Wings for Victory campaign to raise funds for the town's Spitfire. He organised the town's V.E. Day and V.J. parades and service

UXB

On August 30, 1940, a German bomb fell in Albert Quadrant; it was one of three, but this bomb failed to explode and a bomb disposal unit made it safe. It was exhibited at the Tivoli Cinema, which at one time was Weston's Winter Garden Theatre in the Boulevard.

The bomb helped increase the £5,000 fund Weston had promised to raise to buy a Spitfire. £5,000 was completed on 17th October 1940, the people's plane total was mainly raised in shillings and coppers. The Tivoli Cinema itself became a victim from the air raids on the Boulevard area, it was set on fire by incendiaries June 28 1942 and, a day later, was destroyed by a bomb. The site was cleared but redevelopment did not take place on the site until the 1980s when "Tivoli House" flats was built. The development comprised 25 purpose-built luxury flats completed in March 1984.

The end of the war

On 7 May 1945, German troops throughout Europe surrendered unconditionally. With the ending of Nazi rule in Europe, the following day, May 8 1945, was celebrated as V-E Day, "Victory in Europe", Weston held its own V-E Parade Sunday 13 May 1945. The parade started from Ellenborough Park and went through the town, ending with a thanksgiving service in Grove Park.

On May 8, there was dancing in the streets of London when Winston Churchill announced to the nation from Downing Street at 3pm that "The German war is at an end." Britain managed to save its army at Dunkirk, win the Battle of Britain in the air and survive the Blitz. On August 15, Japan surrendered and World War II finally ended. Weston held its own V-J Parade and Service of thanksgiving on Sunday, 19 August 1945.

People and Personalities

Henry Butt

In 1937, Weston was granted borough status and Henry Butt was chosen as its Charter Mayor and also became the first freeman of the town. He was born in 1861 in Langport and died aged 83 in 1944. He was engaged in the coal and timber business and formed the firm of Henry Butt and Co Ltd in 1922. When he sold this he added to his commercial interest by acquiring and developing the Milton Quarries and Lime Kilns. Many of Weston's buildings were built from the quarry's limestone. The large stone houses had individual architectural details that give Weston its Victorian Heritage and links the town to the natural environment.

He was presented with the Freedom of Weston 28 May 1942 and represented the West Ward of Somerset County Council for 25 years.

Henry Butt (Picture, Woodspring Central Library)

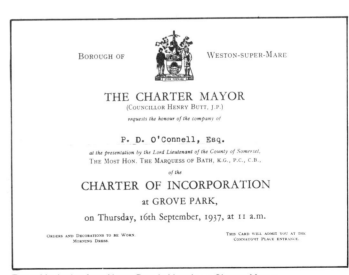

Formal Invitation from Henry Butt in his role as Charter Mayor

Langport House, Eastfield Park, was the home of Henry Butt. The name of the house remains on the stone wall pillar at the entrance.

P.D. O'Connell

Mr P.D. O'Connell of 1 Longton Grove Road, Weston-super-Mare was a former Executive Director of Messrs Mills and Rockley, the well-known outdoor advertising contractors, and group manager of the Bristol Group. He started his publicity life as secretary to the late Mr H.A. Broomfield, manager of the Weston-super-Mare United Billposting Company in Waterloo Street, and, when Messrs Mills and Rockley took over the business, was in charge of the Station Road Office prior to being transferred to Bristol. He was also associated with Mr Broomfield in the management of the former Grand Pier Company. Mr O'Connell was a founder member and subsequent president and chairman of the Bristol and West of England Publicity Club and for seven years chairman of the technical committee of the British Poster Advertising Association. He was also chairman for three years of the South of England branch of the Association.

He was a member of the Town Advertising Association, which in the days of the Weston-super-Mare Urban District Council, was responsible for advertising the town and arranging its entertainments and was the sponsor of the Weston-super-Mare Development Board. In the 1930s, he put forward a scheme to bring light industries to the town and so provide employment for young people instead of their having to look further afield. The scheme was not well received locally and was turned down by the Council, largely on the grounds that it might have a detrimental effect on Weston-super-Mare as a health and holiday resort. Today the Council is doing everything possible to encourage light industries to the town, and one wonders how much more could have been achieved if Mr O'Connell's original scheme had been put into effect.

During the war, Mr O'Connell was a company Commander and Major in the Home Guard, and when it was reformed after Suez was appointed Second in Command of the local force.

He was the founder of the Army Cadet Corps in Weston-super-Mare and its first Commander, in 1941. Amongst other local activities Patrick O'Connell was for 12 years chairman of the Weston-super-Mare Savings Committee.

P.D. O'Connell

P.D. O'Connell and Anthony Eden share a few words together, Mrs Nora O'Connell, Pat's wife at his side in the foreground. As Secretary of State for War in the 1940s, The Rt Hon Anthony Eden asked for local Defence Volunteers to come forward to defend the country during World War II. As a result, the Home Guard was later formed.

"A man for all seasons" wrote the local church on the passing of Mr P.D. O'Connell in 1978. It was recorded that the Bishop of the Dioceses and 18 priests concelebrated the Requiem Mass, shared by a huge congregation. The occasion manifested in a striking way the esteem and affection in which he was held by all who knew him.

The show must go on: Weston's old playhouse was destroyed by fire on Friday, August 21, 1964. The original theatre had 500 seats and was converted from an old Victorian market hall in 1946. The new playhouse, seen here, was built on the same site is a 693 seater theatre; it opened on Saturday July 9, 1969. The first play about the history of Weston, Snow on the Shore, was presented by Weston Dramatic Society at the Playhouse. The play covered Weston's history from 1900 to 1973 and it ran from 27th November to 1st December 1973 with a cast of over 40, including the author of this book. The play was written by Nona Hooper and Bill Clout. The set was designed by John Butler.

1927 waitresses at Weston's Beach Hotel opposite the Grand Pier: to the left of this picture. Elizabeth Emily Brown and her sister Kate take a rest from their duties. They both worked at Weston's Grand Atlantic Hotel where Elizabeth met her future husband, Robert Keyes. This balcony is now part of Madisons fun pub.

Elvis Presley Junior visited the International Helicopter Museum at Weston Airport at Locking Moor Road for a guided tour on Friday 12 February 1993 to look around the unique displays. The American singer was appearing at the Rainbow Club in Bristol. The reason for his visit to Weston was his keen interest in helicopters. I asked Elvis how the first night of his tour had gone the night before, Elvis replied, "Everything went very well, in fact the concert was a sell out, all four nights are a sell out, I am only doing four live shows in the UK. I leave on 15 February to start a world tour." Elvis Junior uses the name Elvis Aaron Presley Junior on his passport, and claims to be the illegitimate son of the rock 'n' roll legend Elvis Presley. At the time of his visit the Bristol Evening Post newspaper wrote – "He has taken blood and lie detector tests to try to counter the cynics who fear an elaborate hoax."

Road racing became a feature in Weston during the 1980s and 1990s. This picture records the Third Wyven 10 Mile Race in 1985. 830 runners made it the biggest field seen in Weston at that time for a road race. Runner no. 90 is the author of this book and went on to run for Weston Athletic Club for two years. The route started at the Tropicana. *(Picture: Weston and Somerset Mercury)*

Weston's Aircraft Heritage

Chocs Away! On 27 August 1993, at the Royal Air Force Town Show, the Western Band of the RAF from Locking Camp entertained large crowds in the summer sunshine. A static display of a life-size Spitfire prototype aircraft was on show, number X4474. The Spitfire, Britain's most famous fighter aircraft, was the symbol of the RAF victory in the Battle of Britain. Displays are always a feature on the beach lawns at Weston. This picture was taken opposite Clevedon Road.

Weston's airfield was opened on 25 June 1936, by the Deputy Lord Mayor of Cardiff, who flew in from Cardiff for the occasion. The airfield cost £56,000 and by the time of the official opening 1,700 passengers had already used it.

In addition to commercial air travel, Weston has many associations with aircraft, both civil and military. There is the nearby Westand helicopter company, the International Helicopter Museum and the Yeovilton Fleet Air Arm Museum plus, of course, Filton and the most famous plane of all — Concorde.

Concorde

The dream of a plane that could beat the sound barrier had been born in Britain way back in 1943 when the Government ordered research into a trans-sonic aircraft capable of flying at 1,000 mph. This was the financially ill-fated TSR-2, but Concorde was the more successful commercial aircraft.

On September 12 1968, Filton's Concorde – 002 – was rolled out to meet the public. Bristol's prized 002 thundered down the runway for her maiden flight on April 9, 1969. Giant Olympus 593 jet engines were chosen to power the aircraft to speeds of 1,450 mph – twice the speed of sound. The prototype aircraft was the first supersonic airliner to be assembled in Bristol. Concorde 002 was built as a research aircraft, not as a passenger-carrying airliner. Together with the French-built prototype Concorde 001, it was used to test and develop all the complex systems and to verify the aerodynamic structural design.The project was originally to have cost £1,137 million, split between Britain and France, but the final figure was a crippling £1.5 billion.

On Bank Holiday Monday, 26 August 1974, the Avon Air Show was held at Weston Airport. Concorde 002 was once more the star of the show, flying at only 50 feet

above the airfield. It made three runs over the airfield, one with its nose dropped, the others in its supersonic flying position. A crowd of 25,000 saw and heard it thunder over their heads. One memorable fly-past saw the pilot reduce the aircraft's speed down to only 180 knots, giving the crowd a lasting memory before 002 went on static display at the Yeovilton Fleet Air Arm Museum.

Concorde thrilled the crowds who were also viewing the event from the platform of Weston Milton railway station which overlooked the airfield with a clear view across the fields. The Red Arrows displayed a special Concorde formation in their routine for the occasion.Concorde underwent more than 5,000 hours of test flights, making it the most tested aircraft ever. Test pilot Brian Trubshaw believes only the Spitfire can equal Concorde for style and engineering achievement.

1994 was the 25th Anniversary of Concorde first taking to the skies. Will the next 25 years see the development and production of "Son of Concorde"?

A Westland 30 helicopter number G-BGHF which seated 6 passengers is one of many different helicopters on show at the International Helicopter Museum situated beside Weston's Air Field. The control tower can be seen in the background. Weston's Airport Control Tower Building is still in full operational use in 1995 although it has not been used for a few years.

How close can you get? Weston-super-Mare Air Day, 26 July 1984. The Red Arrows display above Weston sea front.

The Future for Weston

The fields around this area, once grazed by cows, were waiting further development as part of the Locking Castle house building programme. The Old Locking Moor road route leading into Weston can be seen running right to left of the picture. For the first time, traffic was now using the new Flowerdown Bridge from where this photograph was taken in October 1993.

The nature of things

In 1993, fields formed part of the Locking Castle Housing Scheme and the Motorway Link Road into Weston. In the 1970s the fields, watercourses and their banks were home to the common newt and great crested newt, sticklebacks and minnows, frogs, toads and tadpoles, water boatmen, and dragonflies. There were fieldmice, slow worms, grasshoppers, badgers, rabbits, and adders. Cattle grazed in the fields and the pond life supported swans which returned to nest each year as well as coots, moorhens and ducks. Reed warblers nested in the reeds along with other common and more unusual birds seen in the trees and hedges. The pond was also used by anglers.

Local people have noticed the difference in their gardens surrounding this area, previously visited by blue tits, great tits, wrens, robins, greenfinches, mistlethrushes, chaffinches and butterflies. Swallows and swifts were more rarely seen in the skies.

In 1992/93, the environment in this area changed. By recording the past, people in the future will be more aware that progress has a price that is not only measured in financial terms. Social needs have to meet a growing population and an expanding town needs to grow to meet the challenges that lie ahead in the year 2000. There is a fine balance between social and economic factors that in turn affect the environment in which we all live.

Architecture and Heritage

Visitors to Weston take home with them the beauty of the moment in time but the town's heritage belongs to us all. The buildings of Weston have individual personalities which, over the centuries, have found a creative release in their architecture. Buildings are our largest and most original works of art and they can be judged on their merits for all to see. The sunny climate of Weston brings the town to life, the buildings mirror so much of the town's past history and reflect the way forward into the next century.

"Everything changes, nothing stays the same," said Elizabeth Keyes in June 1991, commenting on Weston's new link road 'system ,stage 1'. The flyover bridge section, length 0.4km spans the railway lines beside Weston's general station in the centre of the town. The new bridge opened that month for the first time to road traffic. It was named the Hildesheim Bridge by Councillor Alan Little, Mayor of Weston-super-Mare, to commemorate the tenth anniversary of the twinning of Weston and Hildesheim in Germany on 16 November 1993.

The seafront bridge is shown awaiting demolition in March 1992. A view from the sea lawns looking towards the Grand Pier and Town Centre. The footbridge was originally built to link up with a development that was never built on the western side of the Dolphin Square Shopping Centre. To the centre of this picture, the clock from the former bus station was resited behind the Tourist Information Centre. One end of the footbridge led direct to the seafront and beach. Both ends of the bridge had different designs.

Weston's Former Beach Lawns Footbridge: the 1967 steel crossing was closed in May 1992. Inspectors said the bridge was dangerous. Pedestrians often crossed the road on foot when the bridge was in use. It became known as 'the bridge to nowhere' as it was little used and it was quicker to cross the road by foot. Demolition started in October 1992.

Weston's Former Beach Lawns Footbridge: the picture on the right shows the main beam units being removed on 18th October 1992 on a cold and wet morning.

The Heron public house used to be called the Borough Arms, being on one of the boundaries of the Borough. Locking Road runs parallel to the front of the public house. In 1995, Locking Road was still the main road into and out of the town. It used to be the site of a beaten track, known as the Watersill, until the Enclosure Act led to the first roads in the town being laid.

Locking Road links into the New Bristol Road and out to the motorway. Traffic congestion, the growing population, and an increasing amount of visitors to the seaside resort has led to the building of the long-overdue relief road, the link up section to the motorway still awaiting completion during this period. The green grass site could be viewed by frustrated drivers who often had to queue at the St Georges roundabout.

Flowerdown Bridge

Completion of Weston's £27 million Link road was due in 1995-96, to link the M5 and the heart of the town centre to help the flow of the resort's 3 million annual visitors. The gap being bridged was over the main railway line adjacent to Weston's airfield to the left. The town centre's road systems will also be improved with this motorway link road, to cope with the increasing holiday traffic, the needs of local businesses, and – last but not least – the local residents.

The new main road route into the resort is designed to end the traffic jams on the busy A370 New Bristol Road and Locking Road. To improve facilities for cyclists and pedestrians in the area, the existing sub-standard A371 railway bridge became part of the cycle/pedestrian network in the area. The Old Locking Moor road bridge was closed to motor vehicles when the scheme was completed and is now used as part of the new cycle/pedestrian route being provided along the northern edge of the Primary Distributor Road between Winterstoke Road and Summer Lane.

In October 1993, one month ahead of schedule and the vital section of the £4 million road bridge across the main Bristol to Exeter railway line was opened. It forms part of the £27 million link road into Weston. The bridge is now joined to the nearby new roundabout at the end of the Herluin Way section of link road which was started way back in 1982. The old Locking Moor Road bridge was closed to traffic at the time of the new dual carriageway bridge opening. The old bridge is situated in the background of the picture.

Weston-super-Mare Primary Distributor Road. The scheme under construction was Summer Lane to the M5, shown on March 13th 1994. The main section is named Somerset Avenue and links Herluin Way to the M5 at St Georges.

The dualling of Herluin Way April 4, 1994: the second carriageway of Herluin Way was under construction to the south of the existing carriageway and involved modifications to the existing junctions at Aisecombe Way, Hutton Moor Road, Searle Crescent and Winterstoke Road. To the north of Herluin Way, the existing footpath in the grounds of Hutton Moor Sports Centre were widened to create a combined cycle/footway.

'The Wind of Change' at Weston-super-Mare's airport: this oversees the road building programme. Memories of the past are still present in this 1993 picture of the airport pillbox from World War II and a wind direction sock that had seen better days.

The Tropicana

The Tropicana was closed to the public when this picture was taken on 20 March 1993 as work was being carried out as part of the phase 1 development, featuring superb new bar and restaurant facilities that opened in Easter 1993.

The panoramic railway layout had been in the town for more than 30 years, 20 of which was spent in the former Theatre building at the Marine Lake and the last ten years at the Tropicana. The model railway had been improved many times over the years. It attracted 20,000 visitors every summer while at the Tropicana.

People of all ages recalled with fond memories or experienced for the first time the pleasure of the speeding model trains going about their business in harmony with the scenic landscape. The lease for the model railway had only a few weeks left to run at the Tropicana, before it expired.

To the right of this picture is the entrance to the model railway exhibition which had 28 trains on 12 tracks running through scenic landscape. This exhibition was housed in the Tropicana after the Marine Lake storm damage and clearance was undertaken when the former model railway building was pulled down. When the Tropicana opened again large crowds enjoyed the new look facilities. At the end of September 1993 the lease for the first floor room that housed the model railway which measured 36 feet by 16 feet was not renewed. The company who manage the centre wanted the space for a change of use for the room.

A new world beneath the waves – the Weston Sealife Centre. Pictured during construction, 29 December 1994.

The Sealife Centre

On September 26, 1994. Next day, work began on the £1.5 million Sealife Centre on Weston's seafront opposite Ellenborough Park between the Grand Pier and the Tropicana.

Knightsbridge Island – the future!

The Knightstone swimming baths closed in 1992 when the £3 million new swimming pool at the Hutton Moor Leisure Centre Complex was due to open, but because of early problems with the water quality, delays left Weston without a swimming pool. Happily, the matter was solved after a couple of months and the new pool is very popular and successful. The only buildings open on the Knightstone Island in April 1995 were the Harbour Inn, situated in the front part of the Knightstone Theatre building, and Weston Bay Yacht Club founded in 1934. Still in full use were the car parking areas, motor boat trips and mooring for boats in the harbour. Knightstone Island still awaited redevelopment plans.

Weston's Model Village

The landscaped gardens had a model of a country town and surrounding district with a castle, windmills, waterfalls, a cottage and a manor house. It was built on the site proposed by the Borough Council for the east-west road to the sea front.

At first, the County Council only agreed to a five-year lease. The road, however, was not built and as a result the lease was later extended. Originally the land had been leased to the private company by the Royal Hotel in 1961, and the village was ready to open in 1962.

The manager of the model village from 1973 – 1982 was the late Mr Robert Spurling Snr. Jonathon Spurling took over the business in 1982 and improvements were made to attract the visitors. Remote control boats caught the eye of the passer-by on the sea front. After 24 years on the sea front, the model village was put up for sale and, in 1986, it was dismantled and the land on which it was built was used for an extension to the Hotel car park.

Parts of the model village still exist today; its new home is in a woodland setting beside the Kewstoke end of the Toll road.

The former location of Weston's model village was on a half-an-acre site on the sea front. The village cost £10,000 and was situated between the Royal Hotel to the left and the Winter Gardens to the right.

Weston's New Skyline – 17 June 1992. Weston's first hotel – the Royal Hotel – pictured in the centre foreground oversees all the changes around it. The New Town Square and Sovereign Centre which opened that year make a fitting backdrop to this view taken from the sixth floor of Weston.College. The site of The Royal Hotel was part of the original master plan to develop Weston. The Hotel has undergone many changes since it opened in July 1810. The Hotel stands on the site of a farmhouse which was destroyed by fire in the late eighteenth century. It was given its title after the Prince of Wales, later to become King Edward VII, had stayed there for a night.

Remembering the past to improve the future

The loss of the former Owen & Owen shop's Oolitic limestone facade which once stood on the site was mourned at the time. However, the new building carried on the theme and style of the type of development needed when buildings are replaced so that they blend into their environment and make the town more attractive architecturally. Generally, people who commented on the new building were pleased with the result. The original shop was founded in 1860 by Arthur Butter, his son ran the drapery store which was known as B.T. Butter. Colmers of Bath took it over in the early sixties. In 1973 Owen & Owen became the last company to trade from the historic building, from 1973 to 1993.

Ninety staff lost their jobs when the four storey historic building closed. Some of the staff had been with the store for 40 years. The store closed because the Owen & Owen company said it was too small for its future needs. The company had also closed its store in Bath.

A Building Society bought the site and built a financial services unit and a shop. The development of the new building provided new jobs after the closure of one of Weston's oldest department stores.

'**Gowen, Gowen Gone.**' – the Owen & Owen store, 23 January 1993. This was the first day of permanent closure and the shop waits for demolition a week later.

New jobs for old: this picture shows the purpose-built replacement for the Owen & Owen store, photographed in Spring 1995.

A Shopin there, a shopin here. Weston new look High Street, 20 March 1993. What a site Owen & Owen was – the foundation stones now laid for a new shopping era. To the right of the picture is the Woolworth building which has overseen the recent changes. The Sovereign Shopping Centre was 11 months old when the picture was taken and well established.

Wadham Street Baptist Church

During the Second World War the whole of the premises sustained damage by bombing during a 1941 air raid (see the 'Weston at War' section of this book). Temporary repairs were made which enabled the building to be used again. The wartime bomb damage led to a modern complex of church and meeting rooms being built behind the original Victorian facade.

The church was put up for sale in the 1980s, partly due to falling attendances and increased running costs. In 1985 a local building restoration trust called the Weston Trust bought the redundant church to save it from demolition and the redevelopment of the site. The trust, an independent charity, was formed to preserve the resort's architectural heritage.

Building work started in the mid-1980s through to the early 1990s to convert the old church into a top arts centre. It was renamed the Blakehay Arts Centre. The Centre was named after the old village Blakehay field which lay between High Street and Wadham Street in which the church was built. The Centre caters for local arts and social events. There is a 250 seat auditorium, with a low level apron stage and raked seating.

A former schoolhouse next door has room for rehearsals and events seating up to 80 people. Future generations have the Weston Trust to thank, plus the many volunteers and builders on employment training and the trust's own work experience scheme, for bringing this historic building back into use. This is truly a centre to benefit the people and town of Weston-super-Mare, made possible by the people who have a love for the town. The past was saved for the future.

Wadham Street was built on Smyth-Pigott land and named after the Rev Wadham Pigott, the Lord of the Manor. The Reverend Wadham Pigott lived in Grove House, Weston. He came to Weston as curate in charge of the Parish Church in 1790s, later becoming the Squire and philanthropic benefactor of the town of Weston-super-Mare. Wadham was the first member of the Pigott family, being Lords of the Manor, to live permanently in Weston. His influence was such that he played a major role in changing the town from a small village into a holiday resort.

Wadham Street Baptist Church was built in 1850; 10 years later it was to be remodelled by famous local architect, Hans Price who designed many of Weston's finest Victorian buildings .The design gave the church its distinctive frontage.

250 seats were to be fitted shortly after this picture was taken. The restored seats were the original church chapel seating. The chapel has now become the auditorium. Tests were under way for the fitting and securing of these seats. Blakehay Centre was later among the buildings which took part in the European Heritage Days and were opened for the public to view on 11 and 12 September 1993. Renovation work was still in process at this time, sponsors could contribute towards the costs of installing the tiered seats.

Time zone for the next Millenium

Christmas Eve 1993: The Weston Sovereign Shopping Centre clock installed when the centre opened in 1992 records the passing of time. As time changes so does everything around it. The clock works on a complex system of pneumatics and hydraulics, being the mechanics used to work the eight puppet figures which play one of a hundred tunes stored when chiming the hour. The clock has a life expectancy of ten years.

April 1996: Weston to return to Somerset!

Many Westonians have felt that Weston belongs in Somerset. Yet, under the previous Local Government reorganisation, Weston had sat uncomfortably in the 20-year-old Avon County Council. In 1994, this came to an end with the proposal to replace Avon with four unitary authorities. Woodspring was to be renamed as North West Somerset, and Avon County Council itself was to be abolished.

BEST PUB WALKS IN GWENT – Les Lumsdon *(£6.95)*

PUB WALKS IN POWYS – Les Lumsdon & Chris Rushton *(£6.95)*

BEST PUB WALKS IN PEMBROKESHIRE – Laurence Main *(£6.95)*

More Pub Walks . . .

There are many more titles in our fabulous series of 'Pub Walks' books for just about every popular walking area in the UK, all featuring access by public transport. We label our more recent ones as 'best' to differentiate them from inferior competitors!

Explore the Lake District:

100 LAKE DISTRICT HILL WALKS – Gordon Brown *(£7.95)*

LAKELAND ROCKY RAMBLES: Geology beneath your feet – Brian Lynas *(£7.95)*

FULL DAYS ON THE FELLS: Challenging Walks – Adrian Dixon *(£7.95)*

PUB WALKS IN THE LAKE DISTRICT – Neil Coates *(£6.95)*

LAKELAND WALKING, ON THE LEVEL – Norman Buckley *(£6.95)*

MOSTLY DOWNHILL: LEISURELY WALKS, LAKE DISTRICT – Alan Pears *(£6.95)*

THE THIRLMERE WAY – Tim Cappelli *(£6.95)*

Cycling . . .

CYCLE UK! The essential guide to leisure cycling – Les Lumsdon *(£9.95)*

OFF-BEAT CYCLING IN THE PEAK DISTRICT – Clive Smith *(£6.95)*

MORE OFF-BEAT CYCLING IN THE PEAK DISTRICT – Clive Smith *(£6.95)*

50 BEST CYCLE RIDES IN CHESHIRE – edited by Graham Beech *(£7.95)*

CYCLING IN THE COTSWOLDS – Stephen Hill *(£6.95)*

CYCLING IN THE CHILTERNS – Henry Tindell *(£7.95)*

CYCLING IN THE LAKE DISTRICT – John Wood *(£7.95)*

CYCLING IN LINCOLNSHIRE – Penny & Bill Howe *(£7.95)*

CYCLING IN NOTTINGHAMSHIRE – Penny & Bill Howe *(£7.95)*

CYCLING IN STAFFORDSHIRE – Linda Wain *(£7.95)*

CYCLING IN THE WEST COUNTRY – Helen Stephenson *(£7.95)*

CYCLING IN SOUTH WALES – Rosemary Evans *(£7.95)*

CYCLING IN NORTH WALES – Philip Routledge *(£7.95)* ... *available 1996*

Sport . . .

RED FEVER: from Rochdale to Rio as 'United' supporters – Steve Donoghue *(£7.95)*

UNITED WE STOOD: unofficial history of the Ferguson years – Richard Kurt *(£6.95)*

MANCHESTER CITY: Moments to Remember – John Creighton *(£9.95)*

- plus many more books being regularly added to our list.
All of our books are available from your local bookshop. In case of difficulty, or to obtain our complete catalogue, please contact:

Sigma Leisure
1 South Oak Lane, Wilmslow, Cheshire SK9 6AR
Phone: 01625 - 531035   Fax: 01625 - 536800

ACCESS and VISA orders welcome – call our friendly sales staff or use our 24 hour Answerphone service! Most orders are despatched on the day we receive your order – you could be enjoying our books in just a couple of days. Please add £2 p&p to all orders.

We publish guides to individual towns, plus books on walking and cycling in the great outdoors throughout England and Wales. This is a recent selection:

General Interest

MILDRED SMITH'S TRADITIONAL RECIPES – in conjunction with Granada TV's Main Ingredient programme *(£4.95)*

EXERCISES THAT WORK FOR YOU: NON-STRENUOUS FITNESS BASICS FOR BODY, MIND AND SPIRIT – Elizabeth Graham-Smith *(£6.95)*

TRAINING THE LEARNER DRIVER – Don L. Gates *(£6.95)*

FORGOTTEN DIVISIONS: THE FIRST WORLD WAR FROM BOTH SIDES OF NO-MAN'S LAND – John Fox *(£7.95)*

MYTHS AND LEGENDS OF CORNWALL – Craig Weatherhill and Paul Devereux *(£6.95)*

Southern Walks and Cycle Rides

PUB WALKS IN THE MENDIPS – Rod Lawton *(£6.95)*

PUB WALKS IN CORNWALL – Laurence Main *(£6.95)*

BEST PUB WALKS IN NORTH DEVON – Dennis Needham *(£6.95)*

PUB WALKS IN SOUTH DEVON – Laurence Main *(£6.95)*

CYCLING IN THE WEST COUNTRY – Helen Stephenson *(£7.95)*

BY-WAY TRAVELS SOUTH OF LONDON – Geoff Marshall *(£6.95)*

BY-WAY BIKING IN THE CHILTERNS – Henry Tindell *(£7.95)*

RAILWAY RAMBLES: London and the South-East – Clive Higgs *(£4.95)*

BEST PUB WALKS AROUND CENTRAL LONDON – Ruth Herman *(£6.95)*

BEST PUB WALKS IN ESSEX – Derek Keeble *(£6.95)*

LONDON BUS-TOP TOURIST – John Wittich *(£6.95)*

TEA SHOP WALKS IN THE CHILTERNS – Jean Patefield *(£6.95)*

Further afield. . .

FIFTY CLASSIC WALKS IN THE PENNINES – Terry Marsh *(£8.95)*

EAST CHESHIRE WALKS – Graham Beech *(£5.95)*

WEST PENNINE WALKS – Mike Cresswell *(£5.95)*

RAMBLES AROUND MANCHESTER – Mike Cresswell *(£5.95)*

YORKSHIRE DALES WALKING: On The Level – Norman Buckley *(£6.95)*

WELSH WALKS: Dolgellau /Cambrian Coast – L. Main & M. Perrott *(£5.95)*

WELSH WALKS: Aberystwyth & District – L. Main & M. Perrott *(£5.95)*

WALKS IN MYSTERIOUS WALES – Laurence Main *(£7.95)*

RAMBLES IN NORTH WALES – Roger Redfern *(£6.95)*

CHALLENGING WALKS: NW England & N Wales – Ron Astley *(£7.95)*

PUB WALKS IN SNOWDONIA – Laurence Main *(£6.95)*

BEST PUB WALKS AROUND CHESTER & THE DEE VALLEY – John Haywood *(£6.95)*